HERMAN®
For Pet Fanciers

SHELDON PRESS
LONDON

First published in the United States of America in 1982 by
Andrews and McMeel, Inc., a Universal Press Syndicate
Company, Fairway, Kansas

First published in Great Britain in 1983 by
Sheldon Press, SPCK, Marylebone Road, London NW1 4DU

Second impression 1985

British Library Cataloguing in Publication Data

Unger, Jim
  Herman for pet fanciers
  1. American wit and humour, Pictorial
  I. Title
  741.5′973   NC 1429

  ISBN 0–85969–387–2

Printed and bound in Great Britain by
William Clowes Limited, Beccles and London

"I told you not to wear that dumb hat."

"You'll have to come back later.
They're not biting!"

"How far can I send this cat for 30 dollars?"

"Whaddyer mean, 'put him outside'?
I can't even move."

"He wants this book on witchcraft."

"He's got my tuna fish sandwiches again!"

"Stop him! He's got your dinner."

"Is this the first time he's been
outside today?"

"I've lost the use of my legs!"

"I'm sorry — I don't have any cream."

"Where's that dumb cat?"

"Is my portable TV in there again?"

"Now don't mention coming in here
when we get home."

"He's half parrot and half homing pigeon. I've sold him ten times!"

"Did you tell the dog he couldn't
go out tonight?"

"Your wife told me you
sold the pet crocodile."

"I've been down here before! Watch
out for the little guy in the fur coat."

"Downstairs . . . eight letters . . .
starts with 'B'."

"Who left the stereo switched on?"

"See, I told you daddy only
had a 'concussion.'"

"Can I borrow some of your after-shave?"

"If you buy a goldfish, I'll throw in
the aardvark."

"I told you it was a dog movie!"

"We haven't seen a duck for two hours!"

"I keep the door locked. I can't understand
how they all got in there!"

"He never said that! I saw your lips move."

"Can I exchange this for 'Doggo-Chunks'?"

"Have you got a room with bars
on the windows?"

"He really likes you!"

"He hates it when someone uses his bowl."

"Those two seem to be enjoying
themselves."

"See what happens when you have too many walkies!"

"I wish you'd wear a hat in there. I've been
looking all over for you."

"You left that back door open again."

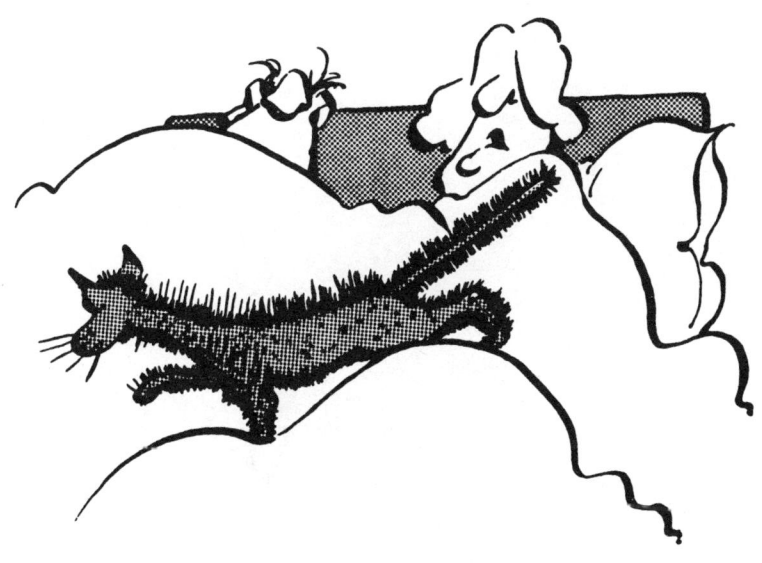

"He's chewed through the TV cord again!"

"I told you that was HIS chair!"

"I never did like dogs!"

"SIT!"

"I need a tropical fish,
18 inches by 9½ inches."

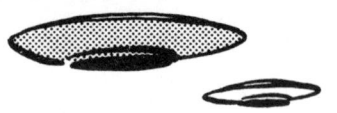

"We flew over one of your cities on
the way in ... very impressive!"

"He's not walking backwards; you've got
the leash on the wrong end!"

"Your dinner's getting cold."

"Don't overfeed the fish, nag, nag, nag."

"Don't be a spoilsport! Guess who it is."

"When I said you could have your friends over for lunch, I meant humans."